WIDOW

Widowland

PAMELA MANCHÉ PEARCE

Green Bottle Press

First published in 2018
by Green Bottle Press
83 Grove Avenue
London N10 2AL
www.greenbottlepress.com

Cover design by Økvik Design
Cover image © Viviana Gonzales
Author photo by Shana Schnur
Typeset by CB editions, London
Printed in England by Imprint Digital, Exeter EX5 5HY

ISBN 978 1 910804 12 4

In memory of Barre W. Littel,
with gratitude for the love we shared
and the life we lived.

Grateful acknowledgement is made to the publications where the following poems, some in earlier versions or with other titles, have appeared: *The Cancer Poetry Project 2*; *Hospital Drive*; Hudson Valley Center for Contemporary Art's 'Between I and Thou' exhibition compilation; *The Westchester Review*; *The Widows' Handbook: Poetic Reflections on Grief and Survival*.

'Structural Damage' is a collage poem with, in addition to my own writing, material from: Knight's *Modern Seamanship*, 12th edition, Commodore R.S. Wentworth; *Living Together Beautifully*, Alexandra Stoddard; *Simple Abundance: A Day Book of Comfort and Joy*, Sarah Ban Breathnach; *May I Walk with You? Courage and Comfort for Caregivers of the Very Ill*, Joyce Hutchinson and Joyce Rupp.

'Gigi, Perhaps' is a found poem using only language from Colette's novella, *Gigi*.

My thanks to:

Amy Holman, my teacher, mentor, and intuitive guide for her invaluable encouragement.

Sharon Israel Cucinotta, Patricia Paine, Johanna Reiss, and Emily Wollman for long, rich friendships that have given me so much support.

Jennifer Grigg, Editor, Green Bottle Press, with deep gratitude for the opportunity to transform an assortment of poems into the longed-for reality of *Widowland*.

Contents

Tree of Cardinals

I stand
in my dead husband's
study and look
out the window
at an expanse
of winter.
I focus
on a small
bare tree,
a tree
of bones.

I imagine
a cardinal
there,
an ornament
on the barren
branches.

A voice tells me
I can have
a cardinal
and one appears.

Then it says
I can have
as many cardinals
as I want.

I imagine another
and it appears

then another
and another
until the
tree is ablaze
with small
crimson
birds.

What is red?
What is red to me?
Everything that blood is.

Red is the fabric   *Childhood,*
apple stitched onto
my first-day-of- school
dress,
and the real one
my grandfather has
shined
for my teacher.

It is the color of his /   *Adult*
cracked fingertips
that smell of   *Smell*
gasoline as he
cups my face to
kiss my hair
goodbye.

I have
as many cardinals
as I want.

Darling

Blue eyes open
flesh shockingly cool
lumpy under the skin
like soft rocks in a fur bag.
I pressed my hand
against his heart, to be sure.

The big cat walked around
the body of the kitten,
tracing its great plume tail.
Howling, growling at this
abyss where his loved one
slipped that morning.

The dead had been the pet's pet.
Hissed and spat at,
then carried by the nape
by his new male mother.
Groomed by his tongue,
nudged to bowl and box.

They yelled
they licked
they leapt and cuffed
without a claw.
They pounced and played
and called out to hunt at dawn
with no prey but the water bowl.

Now he's silent, sniffing
the dying place,
scanning the loops of carpet
for the vivid scent
that was his living love
and home.

Over and over he rubbed his cheek,
eyes closed, belly to the floor,
front legs outstretched
claws dug into pile
as he pressed closer, closer.

I watched it play out,
on the living room
wall-to-wall,
just feet from the spot
where I once, in a hospital bed,
spent a morning spooning,
then losing the beat and breath
of my one,
my heart, my home.

Foxed

I find a dead fox in my garden.
It's one of those winter days when the ground crunches as you walk
    and the sun,
        like a cataracted eye,
        tries
        behind a tight membrane of winter sky.

I look down at the fox.

I know. I don't know. I know.

    / I'm in a flip-book \
        of fox memories
            snapping fast.

Is he one of the kit of kits I saw on a heat-hazed August afternoon?
In light a wash of topaz
they were so cute in their bright
        coats and long black gloves   leaping up, pouncing down
           like cats but with little dog bodies all fluff and vigor.
The whole scene golden: the fur
           the sun going down
           the dry grasses
           and easy, liqueury breeze.

Then I saw him once in the driveway
big as life   sunning himself, ruddy fur rippling,
        black boots and paws swaying from side to side
        as he rubbed his back into the gravel,
        mouth open,
        those sloe-eyes closed in ecstasy.
That one time.

I don't need him anymore.
A stone.
In the afterlife now.
Maybe the inky velvet and indigo sluice of Venetian canals
takes him home
        to somewhere.
Or a quivering length of ruby satin
lowers
 him
 into
 the safe center
 of the earth.

Or something else.   To a dark place?

        Or light?

What do I know

about the afterlife of a fox?   What do I know about the afterlife?

I say goodbye
to the Prince of Trouble
at my feet.   His fur a bristle of rust.
                His plume tail gnawed
                to rope.

  Then from my shovel's tip where his loose legs tremble in space

  his story changes quickly from a romance
  to matter.

And his tooth, once a scimitar, becomes a comma
of yellow bone.

I don't know. I know. I don't know.

Pantoum

My life includes a tragedy,
simply by loving that one man.
It's never over and cannot be understood.
Yes, there was joy and sorrow, too.

Simply by loving that one man
in sickness and in hell. I was no hero.
Yes, there was joy and sorrow, too.
I'll always remember the details.

In sickness and in hell, I was no hero.
There were moments of romance and terror.
I'll always remember the details.
What we suffered's been locked up.

There were moments of romance and terror.
No one ever asked me the details,
what we suffered's been locked up.
Thank God I never had to tell it all.

No one ever asked me the details,
his life was more than a mere tale of horror.
No one wants to hear a story about dying.
I slept beside his bed. The cancer worked on.

His life was more than a mere tale of horror.
Others worked around us, not in it with us.
I slept beside his bed. The cancer worked on.
Days went by, too fast, too slow.

Others worked around us, not in it with us.
Living kept on in the faces of family and friends,
days went by, too fast, too slow.
His dying consumed us, as had our love.

Living kept on in the faces of family and friends,
we didn't know when the moment would come.
His dying consumed us, as had our love.
We had kisses, and the morphine drip.

We didn't know when the moment would come.
But I had no escape from being left behind.
We had kisses, and the morphine drip.
I couldn't avoid the tragedy.

I had no escape from being left behind.
It's never over and cannot be understood.
People like me always go on.
My life includes a tragedy.

Respite

I find my way into an underground jazz club, down and down
into a dark red room, shuddering with the city that surrounds it.
Here, black men hold silver and gold in their hands.
I breathe. I rest my head on the fake red-leather banquette,
    listen,
let all the nights, hours, sets I've spent in clubs like this
    love me back.
I catch my breath after a sax solo, think: How can I be here?
Because 'it's good for me,' to get out and remind me I'm alive.
I have a night off from my husband's dying.
I am working with the drummer as he says something
    to my aorta
that is blood knowledge they own together.
Then, a bossa nova beat insinuates itself into me,
    I am a dancer in a chair.
Conga hands shadow on the drum skin
like the beating of birds' wings
ascending too fast for my eye to see.

Stalker

Four a.m. he
barks me
fast into white,
cold wide awake.

Dripping his acid drool,
showing teeth, tarred ruins of bone,
he pants hot and steady
with the fetid breath of asses licked clean.

He drags me from my holiday called sleep.
Curled safely, I thought, as I was tight inside my mother
but now I trade her thumping, bloody broth
for dreams, blurred narratives, where
oceans float giant birds as boats,
their wings become sails of cobalt, lilac, chartreuse.
And my third-grade teacher, Miss Condit,
works in a dry cleaner's shop where
clothes swing around the racks and turn
into carcasses inside the plastic film.
But she doesn't care –
all dolled up with pastel flowers in her hair.

Terror skitters across my unconscious:
I'm old and alone with just a walker
and the stink of piss.

He snarls me to my feet.
Rivulets of sweat, like liquid ice,
streak the pajamas close against my skin.
I wait it out.

Day spreads oh, so, so slowly.
A golden ooze across the sky
shoos away the shadow hound,
a cowering puppy in retreat,
now a mere fleeting spot of remembered dark.

Widow, Falling

Tell me how to live this beautiful life.
Tell me now.

Help me to make bracelets from tin cans
Christmas wrap from toilet paper
and potatoes cut into stars.
A gourmet meal from sautéed dice of pillowcase
    and hot rollers en brochette
to change my watch to an elastic bandage
to drive safely when I am blind
to know when I collapse, how to fall
to read the eyes of strangers when they ask me for change
    to get home
to ask strangers for change so I can get home,
in their eyes, and mine
to know when I am home and how to act when I am there.

Help me when I collapse.

Second Story Sunlight

after Edward Hopper

First story sunlight
tells a tale of the
expected.

On the porch,
beneath a bright sky,
an old lady in a grey
dress rocks with the Bible
in her lap.

And there's the teen,
posing on the rail,
she knows how to pack her bikini
while she's still
wearing it.

First story sunlight,
looking at nothing (you'd think)
being Marilyn in her head.
Shake it.
Make it.
Marry a millionaire.

But the second story sunlight
is the dark narrative
that lurks in the shadow
of that sun.

Look –
Nana's into the Sodom and Gomorrah part,
clicking her knees together inside
her big skirt.
Click. Click. Click.
She's starting a fire
in the gnarly ashes of (you'd imagine)
her abandoned barbecue.

Looking out into space,
past the trees,
at the Tower of Babel.
She's being carried out.
Feels the flames,
feels the muscles of
that Bible-time firefighter
who's got her in the vise
of his big biceps.

Second story sunlight,
that girl would
write a poem
if she could (but how?).
A villanelle
about the influence of Freud
on Alfred Hitchcock.

Thinking about Hawthorne,
night story starlight,
didn't he say:
'What other dungeon is so dark
as one's own heart!'

I Kiss Your Clothes Goodbye

In the other room
the undertakers slide you
(in a diaper and your
blue bedsore boots)
still a little warm, I think,
into the black bag.

I have to set your clothes out
for this trip as I have for meetings
in London and Milan,
for golf outings and visits
to your mother.

I had ten months to do this
(I was busy keeping busy)
and now I am in a rush,
like old times, with a limo
waiting outside.

What does a well-dressed gentleman wear
to have his corpse set afire?

I pick the khaki Nehru jacket,
so chic, so avant,
the one we bought that hot July
on Sunday afternoon
in the Marais when all the other
stores were closed.

And the blue and white checked shirt,
it brought out the color of your eyes.
Now closed forever and hardened like a doll's.
My fingertips drew down your lids,
as soft and velvety
as the sun-warmed petals
of a rose.

Grey flannel slacks,
always in good taste, don't wrinkle much,
and no good WASP would travel
anywhere without a pair.

And underwear? Yes.
Why?
Why any of this?
I kiss the fly of your undershorts,
one last time.

Temple

It might have worked: taking his cremains to the Metropolitan Museum of Art and placing them in the coin and medal cabinet of King George III. Neatly filling, with ash and bits of bone, the one hundred and thirty-five shallow drawers. But I took a wrong turn into The Arts of Africa and Oceania and found the temple of my husband's brain cancer. A repository of so much grief that the life and death forces whistled past me, crying, crying. Portrait skulls and reliquary guardians with bared teeth and hats of turtle shells and mouse bones. Masks howling with human hurt and loss, streaked with soot and mud that smelled like radiation fire. The vacant eyes on a death mask, cleverly stuffed with cowrie shells then stitched down with sinews of pig, then ringed round and round with the red dust of butterflies. Heads. Heads. Heads. My posture never changed even though I saw photos of my dead husband (smiling because he had no idea of his future) strung as ornaments on a necklace for the Oba of Benin. I stood at the base of this volcano of ancient knowledge, waiting with parched flesh for the rush of liquid flame to overtake me. To bring me to my knees as a sacrifice to my original being as a bird, a pebble, a beach. To rush me and his ashes down a river of sorrow and blood.

Gigi, Perhaps

After forty years that are a single sigh,
she pulls on rubber gloves and coolly sets about

her household chores. Honorable habits
of a woman who has lost her honor.

Spring sunshine through the lace curtain,
    she unties her apron,
under which she wears a black dress,

slips her arm through the handle of her shopping bag and
sets off to market.

'The Cobra' at the Olympia does an acrobatic turn
uncurls like a snake. White ostrich feathers froth

around the relentless beauty of her face.
She's Columbine in spangled black tulle,

and a Nile-green Persephone corset with Rococo
rose-embroidered garters. She won't have a savage.

But none of her admirers ever mentioned marriage.
She wants a gentleman.

She wants Italy, the sea, phosphorescent blue flames
in depths of green, emerald's miracle of elusive blue.

Hummingbirds in flowers, love under gardenias
in full bloom beside a moonlit fountain.

In a fraught moment she raised her dotted veil,
her face like a crumpled rose, as a shrug of the shoulders

sent lace quivering with reality. A silly little milliner's
    shop girl
all she could ever be.

In This Life, My Life

I am dirty and fragile,
precious
and tattered,
feisty and eventful.

In this life,
my life,
my body earns secrets
to hold onto,
until its end.

With shattered slippers
the color of tree bark,
limousines,
I kick corpses,
modify ghosts.

My gut, an empty fist
opens and clenches,
with each fresh
course of rage.

I liberate my teeth,
dangerous white bones
in such a pretty row,
strike-force of smile.

My beauty, a gorging feast
for all the blows
and twisting
narrowly endured.

The grey sea churns, huge
and heavy,
as it listens.
I listen, too.

My TV Family

Tim Gunn guided me
like a contestant
on *Project Runway*:
'Make it work!' he said.
I did and mashed
morphine into banana.
'Carry on!' he directed.
I did. I called hospice.
I rode shotgun in ambulances,
like Katie Couric in Darfur.
If she can do it, I can.
I would have called *Mad Money*,
if I'd had the time.
'I need to learn the lingo of finance.
What should I do, Mr. Cramer?
The market's crashing.
Our money and my man are dying.
I can't stop it.
I can't stop it from happening to me.
To us.'
Dr. Oz gave me answers
about how a person dies.
The real, hard scientific facts.
About how a body works and
how it stops working.
Oprah showed me
a strong woman.
Her husband never died.
She had no husband.

But I did.
One moment he was alive
and there were two of us in the room,
the next moment: one person and a body.
A body which he left for me to have.
The sun sets as the moon rises.
My husband is dead and the TV
comes alive.
I am never alone now.
I watch television
in the living room,
where the hospital bed was.
I sit in the big house
in the big chair
and watch the big TV.
At bedtime I take a Xanax and go
to *The Office*.
I am not old.
I am not alone.
I am not a widow.
I am wearing pantyhose and a new cardigan.
I am falling in love with my coworker Jim,
and I don't care how many times I answer the phone:
'Dunder Mifflin. This is Pam.'

I Describe My Needlework Nirvana
in the Form of a Pantoum

Hey, look at me: slip-stitching, popcorning, knotting off,
    and chaining on,
crocheting booties for babies and Irish-waving pillows
    for bedheads.
It's me! In the glow of those flame stitches, I've lost all my wan.
Thanks, mittens. Thanks, afghans. Now I've tossed out
    my meds.

Crocheting booties for babies and Irish-waving pillows
    for bedheads,
my problem it seems was just overthinking!
Thanks, mittens. Thanks, afghans. Now I've tossed out
    my meds,
I'm happy and mellow and I'm not even drinking!

My problem it seems was just overthinking!
Granny squares and potholders – not snacking or snoozing,
I'm happy and mellow and I'm not even drinking!
Bargello this time, or Tunisian lace, perhaps?
    All good whichever I'm choosing.

Granny squares and potholders – not snacking or snoozing,
It's me! In the glow of those flame stitches, I've lost all my wan,
bargello this time, or Tunisian lace, perhaps? All good
    whichever I'm choosing.
Hey, look at me: slip-stitching, popcorning, knotting off,
    and chaining on!

Moment

How do I nail this morning forever?
Can I go again? How many more times
will I be invited to this show?

The earth's exhale,
a haze of pink confetti
tumbling petals like
a cloud of amethyst dust
that floats above
forsythia tossing
yellow flames.

Everywhere, aroused blossoms palpitate
against the wet-on-wet
branches saturated black.

A magician's wand flicks a bouquet from its tip
Voila! with just a tap.
What is this pink black magic?
Are these pastel explosions the orgasms of trees?

Structural Damage

Tropical cyclones are the most destructive of all storms
         My husband has terminal lung cancer
         and seven months
         to live.

with rainfall which brings intense destruction
         If I could plan a creative excursion to go browsing in a
         décor shop, perhaps that would help

that causes the loss of many ships at sea.
         The police called. My son is dead.
         Drove his motorcycle into a tree.
         It was instant. Complete.

     As sure as caring for our homes can be an expression
of our authenticity.   *Cyclones along coastlines have
destroyed cities, some never to be rebuilt.*
     After my father's funeral, my little girl sat in my lap and
announced,

         'I'm fat.'
         (with grief)
   I stopped   our Sunday night ritual
of making soufflés with our children.

Ships at sea should make every effort to avoid a tropical cyclone.

         I began to scream at the top of my lungs
         in the hospital cafeteria,
         pulled my hair out at the roots
         and collapsed on the floor.

In passing through such a storm, wind and sea are most certain
to bring about some structural damage.
Even a well-found ship in some cases may be in danger of
foundering from the extreme violence of wind and sea.

I was only three months pregnant when the labor pains began.

Personnel may be lost overboard or injured by objects adrift
ordinarily considered secured.

I felt a drop, heaviness inside me.

> There was no blood.
> A D&C removed any vestige

of the baby from my womb.

But I realized that dressing for dinner wipes away the stresses
of the day
    and creates an attractive climate for a nice evening together.

Lifeboats, airplanes, and other exposed objects
are most certain to be carried away by the wind and sea.
Many ships at sea have never encountered a tropical cyclone;
if ordinary precautions are used
> What is bleak in life is already obvious.
> I make a conscious effort to point out
the positive in every situation.

> It makes life look brighter.

most ships should never have to pass through a violent one.

McQueen's Last Dresses

Coffins stood round, like open presses,
That shaw'd the dead in their last dresses . . .
   – Robert Burns 'Tam o' Shanter'

I like it when you spread your skirt's lips
Open
with skeletal fingers.
Slide me down your knob of skull,

your face
strapped into a mask of red leather.
Your neck
a tattoo of red lace pulled
tight.

My beads, a million red drops
of glass
slip past your cool shoulders,
my fringe descends, spills
down your breasts
parted into strands by your
hard nipples.

I roll over your curves easily,
swish the backs,
fronts,
insides of your legs
as you prance the runway.

Toward a circle made for fire.
Whoosh of flames surrounds us.
I melt in drops that could be blood
beside your blackening feet.
As fire licks and hisses higher,
the audience, wild,
watches us with horror and joy
as we go down together,
a jumble of seared flesh
and unstrung beads that skitter
across the burning floor.